Ode to a Titty

Poems of life, love and laughter

by Rebekah Simpson

FOREWORD

BY KAREN VERRILL
Founder of Ladies in Pink Scarves and Centre Head of Maggie's Newcastle

I first met Rebekah in December 2009 when she was diagnosed with breast cancer at the age of 38. She was already a mother to three beautiful daughters and was eight weeks pregnant. I was her clinical nurse specialist at the time and, in the eight years since then, have had the privilege of getting to know Rebekah, Mark and their lovely family.

During the pregnancy, Rebekah had a mastectomy and chemotherapy finishing this phase of treatment just a few weeks before Archie, her precious son, came into the world, perfectly healthy and the image of his dad! Rebekah and Mark truly had their work cut out. She had to juggle the hard job of being a mother to the new arrival, looking after her daughters and completing seemingly unending additional cancer treatments: four Weeks of radiotherapy; 18 Herceptin infusions, one every three weeks; another mastectomy to try and reduce the risk of cancer on the other side and then bilateral breast reconstructions. This would be an extremely intensive and tough treatment programme for anyone.

Rebekah had a short spell of the "normality" of being a very busy wife and mother. However, it wasn't long before she developed severe back pain. Initially it looked like this was related to her previous reconstructive surgery, but the pain continued unremittingly, gradually worsening until, in 2012, she was diagnosed with secondary spread to her spine.

Since then Rebekah has been on the endless rollercoaster of living with secondary breast cancer. It has spread to her pelvis, her lungs and her brain and as a result she has been on treatment continuously since 2012, receiving courses of different chemotherapy drugs punctuated by blasts of radiotherapy. Rebekah has experienced some of the most distressing symptoms of cancer alongside the debilitating side effects of anticancer therapies while, every day, trying to live a normal and very active life.

During this time, our paths have been intertwined. When she was having treatment at home I became a regular visitor in my role as a community nurse specialist. I remember draining seromas and dressing wounds in the kitchen with the children running around in the background. We had the opportunity to talk for hours and really got to know each other.

In 2011 I moved back into a hospital based post when I was appointed as CNS to support women diagnosed with secondary breast cancer. Rebekah again became my "patient". Then, in 2013 I moved jobs once more to take up my current role as Centre Head in the new Maggie's Centre. Rebekah has been a regular visitor since it opened. We spend quality time together there. We talk about cancer but there is always more than that. We share stories. Of course there is sadness but we laugh a lot too. We have moved beyond a 'nurse/patient' relationship; we are friends.

There have been times when I arrive at Maggie's for my usual 9am start having driven from Whitley Bay and Rebekah will arrive half an hour later, a lady with incurable cancer having

run nine miles from the same starting point. We live on the same street!

We meet up sometimes in passing. One morning I looked out of my window and saw a beautiful and vital young woman walking her children to school. It was Rebekah. I was lost in thought for several moments, transfixed. Looking at her, who on earth could have any idea what she is living with and through. To Rebekah cancer is a big part of her life but living is much bigger!

Cancer brings fear to all. But her life is not frozen by fear. She is not living under the threat of cancer and death. She is not losing the joy of living in the fear of dying. She is a wife, a mother, a sister, a friend, an active member of her church. She is helping so many others from so many walks of life. Her charity work, raising money for people affected by cancer. Fundraisers on three of her birthdays and her 10th Wedding Anniversary. The race for life when she finished 8th out of hundreds. She wasn't happy with that she wanted to be first. Rebekah has modelled in two black tie fashion shows that I have organised. She has danced her way along the catwalk in front of a packed house, looking sensational, happy and carefree, showing everyone how it is done. Tens of thousands of pounds have been raised from these events.

In her professional life Rebekah was a teacher, she still is. She has worked with me at the University of Northumbria teaching qualified nurses, specialising in Oncology, about cancer and its treatments. Her role has been to share her personal experience of the disease, ensuring the students get a true perspective of what their 'patients' have to cope with. For Rebekah this means waking up every day for the rest of her life knowing she will never be free from cancer. Her impact on our students cannot be quantified but I know that, because of meeting her, they will be better nurses.

I have asked Rebekah on many occasions, to spend time in Maggie's, with people (particularly young parents) who have been diagnosed with cancer, to share her own unique insight, strength and positivity with them during their own very difficult and testing cancer experience. She has helped countless numbers of people by doing this and made many new friends along the way.

In 2016 I was asked to find someone who has used Maggie's to write, in their own words, what the centre means to them and read it at our Christmas carol concert. My decision was an easy one, Rebekah. She wrote her piece, a poem, and came in to read it to me. I was overwhelmed. It was brilliant. The last time Rebekah had written poetry was when she was 11.

Writing the first poem has been hugely significant because she didn't stop after the carol concert. Poetry breached the dam behind which her thoughts and feelings were constrained and became the canvas on which, with the vibrant colours that run through this book, she could share her thoughts and experiences. With this realisation her words were able to flow from her pen as if driven by some unseen, higher force.

Rebekah herself believes this to be true, that the words are not hers, that someone is giving them to her, that she is being guided, from a higher level, to inspire others, to give them strength in the face of extreme adversity. She calls this higher level, God. Who could challenge or doubt her?

From our conversations I know her faith has always been important. She told me that at the beginning of her journey she turned to her relationship with Jesus for direction and this has kept her going and has allowed her to learn how to live well under extremely difficult circumstances. She believes that God is a real and a tangible presence in her everyday experience.

Rebekah has been to some very dark places, it is inevitable given what she has been through, but she rises from them, turns things around and focuses on the good in her life.

My understanding is that her ability to do this is because of her faith in God coupled with her passionate and fierce love for Mark, her rock, her superhero. She describes this love so vividly in the poem written for him. And of course for her precious children who she, continues to live for and absolutely adores. Rebekah and Mark, as a couple and as parents, have managed to sustain normality and happiness for their children against all the odds and during the toughest of times. Mark has been constant and by her side throughout everything with his supportive and reassuring presence.

It would not be possible to write about Rebekah without mentioning the support she has had from her church and fellow Christians. They have been a huge and very positive part of her life, as have her amazing family and friends. I know she thanks God for them all.

Rebekah and I have always talked, but since she has written this book our conversations have gone deeper than ever before and she has really made me think about my own values, beliefs and much, much more. I have been part of her journey since we met in 2009 but now because of Rebekah, I am on a spiritual journey of my own. It is one that I never expected to be on!

This foreword has been much harder to compose than I had ever considered because there is so much to say about Rebekah, however if I had put it all in, this introduction would be longer than the rest of the book!

She is good, bright, intelligent, kind, compassionate, funny; her sense of humour is razor sharp and sometimes black in the most refreshing way. This is demonstrated by her 'Ode to a titty.' She lost her driving licence and therefore some of her independence because of the cancer, which had spread to her brain, but used the experience in a positive way and wrote about 'her thoughts on the metro'

Rebekah is full of life and full of love. She has a vitality and radiance shining through which Inspires others affected by cancer as well as those not directly affected. She is, courageous, strong, beautiful, resilient and she still has work to do.

She has been through so much that mere words about Rebekah are inadequate; how can I even come close to being able to describe her? How could anyone? However, I am hugely honoured to have been given the job and also that there is a poem about me!

I hope you enjoy this book of poetry written by Rebekah Simpson, an ambassador for the power of the human mind over matter; for inner strength and spirituality and for people everywhere.

Thank you Rebekah.

MY STORY STARTS...

My story starts in 2009, on June 26th I gave birth to the third daughter in our family and in October I discovered I was unexpectedly pregnant with number four. Josie was three and half months old, Evie was two years old and Emma aged seven. Six weeks into the pregnancy I found a lump in my left breast. It was breast cancer, it had already spread into my lymph nodes and needed immediate treatment.

Christmas 2009 was spent preparing for a mastectomy followed by six months of chemotherapy; my pregnancy would be induced so that I could receive radiotherapy. The prognosis was good; most women are cured of primary breast cancer and go on to live full and healthy lives.

This was not to be the journey I would take.

In 2012 I began to suffer with severe back pain and after investigation I was diagnosed with secondary breast cancer in my vertebrae. A whole new chapter of my life began. Secondary breast cancer is incurable; treatment is available to manage the disease, but life expectancy is significantly reduced.

There are no words to describe how completely devastated I was. I had a young family who needed me; there was no place in my life for a terminal illness. I understood that the disease would spread; but no one could say at what rate or where it would show up next. Secondary breast cancer is a 'loose cannon' and has no pattern to its activity or speed of progression. It cannot be predicted or compared with any other person's experience. I faced a future living on a time bomb.

I find myself in 2017 with cancer in my spine,

multiple areas of my bones, my right lung and my brain. Treatment in the form of radiotherapy and chemotherapy has been on-going and continual for five years. It's exhausting, I am physically depleted most days and at times debilitated; my illness is a constant and extreme pressure on my young family's life.

However, my story is not one of doom and gloom. Cancer has indeed altered my whole life but by no means has it ruined my life. The truth is my battle with cancer has transformed who I am for the better and deepened my character beyond my recognition. This in turn has affected the relationships in my life and has miraculously altered my love of life and my love for others. I have a passion to make the most of every opportunity; I demonstrate that no adverse circumstances need ever rob you of hope, peace, love, joy and dreams. Life can hand you lemons this is true, but what you do with those lemons is all down to you.

There have been many painful and anxious times, times I have felt I can't go on, when the grief over the loss of the life I once had and the future I presumed that lay before me, have nearly drowned me. But I have someone in my life who calls me onwards and upwards; someone who loves me beyond all human understanding, someone who has my back covered and my future in hand, someone who leads me through the dark valleys of my life and shows me the way to my mountain tops. This person created my life and is the only person who has the authority to call time on my life; that person is God.

Through my belief in Jesus Christ, God's son, I can daily and in all circumstances access a supernatural realm that empowers me to live my life beyond my human capacity. I put my faith in him and the truth he speaks in the Bible and I am able to combat fear and anxiety and live victoriously in situations that threaten to defeat me.

I am asked over and over again 'How do you remain so strong and hopeful?' It is not positive thinking, I am not Wonder Woman, it is not me at all. It is my total and utter trust in God; I give him all the glory for showing me how to live well and enjoy life without the darkness of cancer obliterating my light completely.

I have no idea what my future holds but if it's as rich and blessed as the last seven years then I have nothing to fear. God has led me to my limits but out of those places have come valuable life lessons and rich fruit. We should all live in the moment, not worrying about what tomorrow brings, making the most of every opportunity we have, but we don't. I have had the privilege of truly facing my mortality which has focused my dreams and placed a value on my life and loves that I could not have grasped any other way.

There are many examples of how and when this has happened one of those is the written word. Pre-cancer I have no history of writing; but in 2016 God unlocked in me a desire to write and I am enjoying immensely the experience of writing my story through prose and poetry. My words and poems will be passed to my children and I hope stand as testimony to my great love for them. If they can also help others then I am happy to publicise them.

I am physically sicker than I have ever been, but in the strength given to me by my Father in heaven I am exploring life and new skills in a greater way than I have ever done. Dreams have been dashed by cancer it's true; but only to be replaced by greater ones. The glory and accolade for this is to be given entirely to God.

I pray that my story and these poems may pique your curiosity to take a step of faith and investigate what it means to have a living active relationship with God. The truth is that your life depends on it; believe me, I know.

Rebekah Simpson

Ode to a Titty

Cancer you chancer, you wormwood, you beast
You dog hole, you maggot, you rancid rat feast
I know your scheme, your evil invention
To destroy my life and defy intervention
Your rabid rogue cells attack all parts of my body
Just 'naff off', make something else your hobby.

Cancer- hey cancer- I'm dying to live
I have so much in my life, so much fight left to give
You've picked a battle with the wrong woman
There's so much defying fire in what's left of MY bosom
I'm gonna kick your ass from here to hell
Ding Dong - 'hey cancer' - 'She's won' sounds the bell.

Go on ravage my organs, try and take control
You may win my body, but never my soul
I have a weapon you cannot break
Strong heart, mind, will, they're not yours to take
My humour, my irony, other tools that defeat you
I can laugh in your face, it's what gets me through

Many giggles I've had from words spoken
I've survived them all and remain unbroken
The inexperienced, insensitive buffoon of a nurse
Probably came out with one of the worst
After she'd stabbed me three times, a cannulation disaster
She hilariously announced 'oh dear, the worst's still to come; removing the plaster'

For my 40th Birthday, my big sister did make
A host of nipple-adorned booby cupcakes
Followed soon after, in her new-found wit
I received in the post two huge knitted tits
Their destination, oh this gives me such delight!
The baps are my boy's cuddlies in bed every night.

Reconstruction a side-aching tale worth reflection
Remaining breast skin stretched weekly
With a silicone injection
Betty Boop baps grow in rounded erection
It's hard to feel a loving connection
To the two cantaloupe melons taking front row projection
The verdict, after closer inspection
I'd rather they faced the same direction

Losing my hair nearly caused me to crack
Someone said 'don't worry dear at least yours will come back
I've not had hair since I was 23'
I gazed into the wizened face of a male OAP
And thought 'shut up' how does that help in my situation?
He looked at me 'what did he want for his worthless HELP?
'A standing ovation?'

Bedroom activity deserves a mention
Or should I say lack of, despite Mark's hopeful intention
Chandelier swinging exists only in memory
Libido, took a vacation
Simply ran off and left me
'Intervention' is needed to create stimulation
My new best friend has battery-operated vibration.

I've come to the end of my little ditty
My bizarre ode sprung from the loss of a much-loved titty
Life can hand you lemons it's true
But what you make from those lemons is all down to you
Look for the stars in the darkest night
Clouds may be hiding them, but they're still shining bright
Look around the problem, the solution is there
Choose life, love and laughter, never lonely despair.

Feel My Love
(for Mark & the children)

When the rain
Is blowing in your face
And the whole world
Is on your case
I long to hold you
In my warm embrace
So you can feel my love.

When the evening shadows
And the stars appear
And I'm not there
To dry your tears
I wish I could be with you
For a million years
So you could feel my love.

I long to make you happy
Be there when dreams come true
There is nothing that I wouldn't do
I'd go to the ends of the earth
And find a way back to you
So you could feel my love.

The storms are raging
On your rolling sea
And on the highway of your loss
The winds of change
Are throwing you wild and free
You WILL see me again
…Just not yet.

Inspired by Adele 'Feel My Love'

My Bulbs

I am so excited
I planted Spring bulbs
And they've actually sprouted.

In order for you to share my glee
I have to tell you
What normally happens to me.

Every plant I try to nurture
Ends up wizened, wasted and withered
Their budding green lives end in murder.

The answer is plain to see
Grow things
That require no intervention from me

The elements are responsible for my bulbs development
Miraculous sun and rain
Create exquisite elegance

My little girl daily down on her knees
Stroking the tiny soft snowdrops
Fluttering and dancing in the February breeze

Each day the two of us with pleasure fill
As we watch blooms burst forth
Rich purple crocuses and golden daffodils

Continuous as the stars that shine
And twinkle on the Milky Way
Along our driveway they grow in never-ending line

I watch them from my window in solitude
A smile breaks on my face
My souring soul is dancing with the daffodils.

Thoughts on the Metro

How would you cope
In the land of the living
If you lived half your life
In the land of the dying?
Come for a whirl in this
Bizarre sensation
This split life creation
That leaves a strange disconnection
When you permanently abide
In this disjointed dimension
Something constantly preventing
A full connection
To the world of the living
And their thoughtless introspection
It's an interesting concept
If not somewhat provoking
Consider it a window to
A caring revelation
At the least-
A moment
For deep reflection.

Quit all the negative stressing

It's one of those days
No singing songs of my creator's praise
I desire that this sorrow be brief
Miles upon miles of grasping greyness
Why is there such length to grief?

It's one of those days
Gates of iron break as time decays
My fortress of steel may not be so strong
A wreckful siege besets my heart
Senseless thoughts are doing me wrong.

It's one of those days
Walking a path of wearying wearing ways
My face is lined with discontent
Will I break in this tortured lament
My soul so alone remains unbent

It's one of those days
Condemned to meditate and gaze
I choose to quit all this negative stressing
No sentence says that my present is my future
I begin to recall all my multitudinous blessings.

The Angel of Maggie's

There is a place
A beautiful place
I love to go there
Waves and swathes of
Warmth and hope wrap their tender
Wings around my bruised heart
My broken mind.

The courtyard wild garden
Swaying with meadow flowers
Banks of bright tulips and daisies
Moving in Spring breezes
My secret healing retreat
Hidden from clinical corridors
A haven from deathly wards and gloomy faces.

I hide amongst the blossoms and blooms
The muted calm colours and secret little rooms
Concerns covered by Summer scents
Gentle faces and voices meant
To offer hopeful choices
In quiet caring soft voices.

Protected, connected, united
With others on the same winding road
All of us candles in the wind
Not knowing where to turn to
When the rain sets in
Trying to hold the shadows at bay
Cancer has caused us to lose our way.

But here in this heavenly place
I come face to face
With a champion fighting my cause
I am a hero within HER heavenly walls
Her compassion drives away my negative perspective
She directs me to a positive objective
She roars like a lioness protecting me
Scaring away the power of illness, setting me free

No one human could achieve this role
Constantly demonstrating such a selfless soul
If she's not human, what is she?
Shall I tell you?
I think..............
She's an angel
I honestly believe this is true.

She's disguised, of course, in heels and smart dresses
Perfect hair and shiny lip glosses
She leaves her white robe in the darkness of the closet
But I'VE seen the tips of her wings
Trailing out from the hems of those designer dresses
Her angel feathers giving my broken heart gentle caresses
Lightening my burden from cancer's stresses
Her white brightness lifts my downhearted face
Bringing supernatural hope to my hopeless case.

Her giggling stories make me laugh
Transforming my darkness into brightness
Carrying my pain on her wings of lightness
Cutting into my dark deepness
Her angelic strength soaking up all my weakness
She's my forerunner, my banner carrier
Waving the flag of victory over my cancer
She's my counsellor, confidante and friend
Living life with me until my end.

She's my guardian angel
Constant, reliable, unchangeable
Always honest never mincing her words
But like a sweet songbird
Giving me reason to hope
And the skills to balance on cancer's tight-rope.

How do I thank this angel of mine?
A few bottles of prosecco, a crate of wine?
I imagine this WOULD cause her eyes to shine
But I think what will cause her wings to flutter in delight
And her golden halo to glow proudly bright
Will be knowing that the strength in HER wings
Are what gave MY wings the chance of new flight.

Quilts of many colours

Back a few years
I am wandering once again
Back to when you littlies started school
I had your special baby clothes
Some generously donated to us
The time had come to put these clothes
to good use.

There were clothes of many colours
I cut them into squares so small
Rompers, dresses, trousers, coats
I made three patchwork quilts
One for each and all

I sewed the squares together
Sewing each piece with love
I made your quilts
Of many colours
That I hoped you'd be proud of

Each outfit held a memory
Of frolics in sun and snow
As I stitched my mind roamed free
To many special moments
So very dear to me.

My lovelies as I sewed
I recalled the story
From the Bible that I read
About a coat of many colours
That Joseph was so proud of

His father deeply loved him
So he gifted Joseph a special coat
These quilts are my gift to you I
passionately hope
That your lives find love and happiness
And I bless all three with a kiss.

I want you to understand
These quilts they are so rich
Full of your mummy's love
Sewed into every stitch
One day you'll know the story
That I loved YOU as I sewed
And that these quilts of many colours
Are worth more than all your clothes.

BOOM

My Life's Passions

Emma Kate your smile lights the room
A gentle spirit that blossoms and blooms
Such a bonny lassy and so amenable
Bringer of reason and always peaceable
Your singing voice will add joy to your life
A positive gift to turn to in times of strife

Evie Rose my strong but fragile flower
Brave and courageous an admirable power
Dwells within your sensitive caring heart
I saw a warrior spirit right from your start
Harness your passion it's a positive force
Embrace your convictions and find your life's cause

My wonderful, cuddly bundle Josie Grace
Sparkly hazel eyes gaze from bewitching freckled face
Brimming with life and bouncing love
The kind heart of an angel sent to me from above
Wherever you go friendship will too
Joy, blessings and love will always follow you

Archie Isaac my bespectacled smiley faced golden haired lad
My singing 'sunny Jim'
who makes me laugh when times are bad
Your dearest treasure 'Rabbit', best pal since birth
Priceless to you, of unfathomable worth
It demonstrates how much loyal love lies deep within
You'll defeat life's adversaries
with your love and beaming grin.

My amazing children, how can it be
That God saw fit to entrust you to me?
But he did, and I handed your lives back to him
Confident that he would one day bring
You all back together united to me
Having won ALL life's battles victoriously

You birds of a feather
Please stick together
Look out for one another
Your strongest allies are your sisters and brother
Direction will be found by seeking God's face
Only in Him will you find true freedom and grace

Real

Mark

Mark, I love that your name
Rhymes with Aardvark
Also with shark
And with Pockmark, hark and quark!?
Sorry, sorry
I'm just enjoying taking the pee
Out of rhyming words that entertain me

Really I am trying to put off
Explaining what you mean to me
As you know, romantic emotions
Make me a tad squirmy
But it has to be said before I depart
There has never been another so dear to my heart

Oh Mark (I might as well go for this)
I love you, I love you
I love you my Mr Almighty
I'm so glad it's YOUR pyjamas
That have ended up nightly next to MY nightie
Don't be mistaken, don't be misled
We actually wear 'nowt' in bed
I HAD to explain this
Cos Mark likes 'FACTS' to be said.

Here we go Mark
You're the rudder to my wayward boat
You're the solid vessel that keeps me afloat
You're the cup that matches my saucer
You're the amazing father to our son and daughters
You're the clear full-stop on my rambling sentence
The warming soul that melts my indifference

Our love has not been a walk in the park
More like sliding slipping and spinning in the dark
Often not sure of the direction we're heading
Or how solid the ground on which we're treading
Our secret 'friendship' we hold tight to each other
We know we were made for one another

Our solid foundation is built on nothing less
Than Jesus and His righteousness
In the darkest days and in times full of joy
Jesus is our peace that NOTHING can destroy
His love for us both has been patient and kind
We can stand united, in his word always aligned

So Mark my 6ft 3 hazel-eyed Ginger Ninja man
My flame-coloured head to our amazing clan
My counsellor, strengthener, repairer,
My forerunner, fire, defender,
My fighter, shelter, helper,
My protector, inspirer, provider,

My friend, confidante, believer,
My companion, explorer, inventor
My buddy, soul mate, instructor
My wonderful, wonderful man
My truly awesome, faithful, constant,
Dependable, hilarious, wonderful man.

When the time comes that we have to part
We can both take great heart
In knowing that 'we will meet again'
In a place full of joy, free from suffering and pain
At those pearly gates we'll greet with great elation
Eternity together, the end of all separation

And there Mark, you will be, at last perfected
No longer by me to be corrected
We'll have made it Mark, married bliss
There's no nagging in utopia, nothing's amiss
So look upwards and higher to a better place
Where our love will be perfected by God's
boundless grace.

Sarah

You have never known life without me
I had only 18 months of life without you
Sliding, careering,
Meandering, flying
Dipping, diving
Weaving and wandering
Pulling each other through
To THIS - our Middle Ages.

Early memories are distant and few
Down in the allotment summery days
Amongst the daisies, daffodils, sweet peas
We sat side by side smiling
In matching summer flowery dresses
And heated haze
Cabbage patch kids
With sweet little faces
That was me and you

The Baptist Church bluebell picking
Swathes of indigo under dappled trees
Bonfires, dunking apples so carefree
Mrs Baxter's sticky treacle toffee
Easter singing with Harry on the organ
'Up from the Grave He arose
With a mighty triumph o'er his foes'
You were always singing with me

Keswick, camping, giggling
In our sleeping bags at night
Made up games of Wonkey Donkey
I can still feel you riding on my back
Practising kissing on each other
And daring each other to 'touch tongues'
Nipping, fighting some vicious attacks
Sibling threats and throw away hurts
But a loyal indestructible love lies
Between You and me

Rain or shine the lake side mountains
Mummy beckoned us and called
Up Helvellyn, High Street, Blencathra
Fog, gales, snow
Sun, vertical rain, all seasons
Windy photographs on blustery peaks
We reached the heights of
Many mountain tops
Always conquered with you and me

The dam at Braithwaite
A favourite location
Dinghies and diving
Ducking and delight
Hours spent in mountain streams water
Straight from freezing springs
Slate houses, pooh sticks under little stone bridges
Summers passed in glorious hue
And none of them spent without you

Christmas, mummy's favourite time
Gifts of dolls and homemade clothes
from her capable hand
Tiny Tears, teeny tiny tears
Teeny weeny tiny tears where would the line end
Mini micro itsy bitsy teeny weeny tiny tears?
Hours we spent with our dollies so dear
Just like us our Tiny Tears cried real tears
We were make-believe mothers
With babies to love and rear
Childish nurturers were you and me.

Love and Marriage
Longed for - found - re found and lost
Babies yearned and desired for brought joy
But unexpected cost
In sickness and in health
We've done it all together
Down to the depths and on mountain tops too
There is NO ONE in my life
Remotely like YOU

Sarah, I could go on and on
There's nothing we haven't gone through
Separation
Misinterpretation
Fights and fall outs
Disappointments, depression
Death of both parents before we were due
Rejection, dejection, disconnection
But always, always and forever supported by you.

Life can be a battle we both know
But we'll stand side by side
Into the next fight we go
Shields to each other offering protection
Loyal, faithful 'Brave Hearts' are we
Our blood runs deep with devoted affection
Sarah, dear Sarah I want you to see
That there will never be a time without a you and a me.

P

Blue Badge Bullies

I was legally accepted
No council member protested
No forms were objected
I'm a rightful member of the Blue Badge Gang.

What do I have to
Do to be respected
What do I do to belong
What do I have to
Do to be connected
With other members of the Blue Badge Gang?

I struggle out of my car to your unwelcome stare
At my lack of wheelchair
'You can't be entitled to THIS welfare'
Shouts an existing member of the Blue Badge Gang

I can only dream
About being respected
I exaggerate my limp and hobble along
It seems my fate is to be
Forever corrected
By other members of the Blue Badge Gang

One day I'll tell you of MY disability
My silent killing difficulty
My deathly cancer the insidious thief of mobility
I am an entitled member of the Blue badge gang

Let me assure you
I'd rather NOT be
In your OAP sickly club
You all look old and I'm still so young
Ironically most of you will outlive me
You judgmental members of the Blue Badge Gang

Your discrimination has taught me
Never to judge what I see
Let's open our minds to the possibility
That many folk carry hidden disabilities

What do I have to
Do to be respected
What do I do to belong
What do I have to
Do to be connected
With other members of the Blue Badge Gang?

I'm the Blue Badge reject
That is forever unprotected
The hidden disabled one that you've all neglected
But I AM a fully pledged rightful member
Of the Blue Badge Gang

The Shadow

I refuse to let cancer's shadow hang over me
Christ came to earth at Xmas to give me the hope of eternity
He brought joy to my world that was tangled and bound
He broke into my darkness and spread love's light around
This gift of hope is a message to my heart
Hope that God loves me whether I'm near my end
or not far from my start.

So why rob my life of this gift of love
Which comes with daily blessings from above?
And dwell on the pain that cancer has given me
Or the time it has robbed from my family
The scars on my body and words spoken of death
Could hang over my life until I take my last breath

But I CHOOSE life and boughs of holly
This IS the season to be jolly
It's the chance to bless and serve others I meet
The sufferers of cancer, or the homeless on the street
And despite my sickness I live free from strife
If I allow this attitude of love to rule my life

Tinsel, Santa, carols and lights
Turkeys, gifts and elves in striped tights
My children chaotically adorn my tree
With candy canes and tinsel so tacky
I love it - I love it all, I love to see them so excited
We've been through so much but we stand united

Runny noses from the chilling sun
Steaming breath from winter fun
Rosy cheeks from frosty days
We warm our hands round the stove's hot blaze
I love to hear their smiles and giggles
Bottoms on my lap as they writhe and wriggle

Thank you God for life's time I've had
The gift of my family through the good and the bad
So I make the most of each treasured day
To live in fear is not God's way
He sent his Son that I may be free
Fear and dread have no grip on me

Some days I dream of other lands way up high
Lands I heard of once in a lullaby
Where sickness has no place and bluebirds fly
Above the rainbow so, why can't I?
But I have a job still to be done
To push through this cancer until my battle is won

To make a trail for others to follow
In paths of hope not of sorrow
To treasure each moment as if it's my last
Xmas is coming I'm having a blast
Not to worry about what's next
No one really knows what to expect

I make the most of Xmas memories
Who knows it could be the last one for me
I make it matter
I battle on my heart WILL not shatter
I turn my eyes and look full in Jesus' wonderful face
Then my troubles on earth simply fall away
In the light of His glory and grace.

So I refuse to let cancer's shadow hang over me
I look to Xmas and what do I see?
I see the 'hope' of eternity.

Under His Wings

Your word is a lamp unto my feet
You call me to walk to the rhythm of your heartbeat
Truth lights my way and I wander no more
On the wings of an eagle, I rise and soar
High above all my fears my troubles cease
The love of the Father, floods my soul with peace.

'Do not be troubled', His gentle voice breathes
Like a whispered breeze amongst the fresh Spring leaves
'Nothing can separate you from my love
Not demons below, nor angels above
Not fears of today, nor troubles of tomorrow
Not disappointments from the past, nor life's future sorrow.'

'Dwell in my sheltered rest
My mighty power your refuge, your true fortress
Covered in my feathers, you nestle under my wings
Your fretful mind slumbers, your soothed soul sings
Of songs of victory, freedom, life's shining light
Oh wonderful Jesus my souls searching delight'

My eyes lift up and my courage grows
Strength and confidence flood and flow
Outwards, upwards, ebbing and swelling
Hope from His Spirit in me deeply dwelling
Trepidation recedes like the turning tide
Perfect love casts our fear no place to reside.

'My dear daughter keep your mind stayed on me
In the power of my name your demons will flee
My only sons arms outstretched on the cross
His face anguished in pain and searing loss
A crown of thorns on His tortured head
A spear in his side where His life blood bled'

All for you, all for you, for you to be free
Jesus died so that you could be joined to me.
Pay Him the honour that He is due
Remember the price He has paid for you
Buried He carried your sins far away
And one day He'll return, Oh glorious day

Find peace in Christ's suffering, it cost God His Son
The price for your purchase, your life's victory won
Be lost no more in anxious bleakness
Speak the truth of his wounds to the depth of your weakness
Rise up child of mine from your knees to your feet
Be transformed in your mind sing songs of defeat

God's word is the answer to victory in life
Read it, soak it, feed on it, walk free of strife
Renew your mind and gird your loins
Not with riches, jewels and costly coins
But with the mighty power of God's living voice
Grab it, believe it, pursue it, your daily choice.

Dwell in His word, the bread of life
It cuts through your thoughts like the sharpest knife
Transforming, transcending, abandoned to Him
Your life renewed in submission, free from sin
Pursuing, passion, persistent of heart
Stand up, stand-out, be set apart

Rise up strong people of God
The trumpet is calling, there's power in the blood
Our Father on high His will be done
Here on earth as in heaven His Kingdom come
Be ready, be ready, our minds clear and strong
One day we'll go home, the place we belong.

UNIQUE

YOU are unique
From your roar to your squeak
From your head to your toe
From your fast to your slow
From your ears to your tears
From your DNA to the words you say
From your heart to each body part
From your blink to your wink
From your fingerprint to the way your eye glints
From the start of your life to the end of your days
You are unique in a trillion ways
YOU are unique
To the God that you seek.

Ward Mouth

The ward mouth knows everybody's business.
The ward mouth knows all the nurses names
And all the nurses boyfriends names
And all the nurses boyfriends mum's names
The ward mouth is known by all the nurses.
They never return to treat her when she's in next time.
The ward mouth knows more than the nurses
The House Doctors and the Oncologists too.
She self-medicates and hates being told what to do.

The ward mouth never gives up
when the system gets it wrong
She just makes medical suggestions
And won't dance to their song
If she needs to, she'll defy the system
And would never allow her-self to be the victim
The ward mouth knows her own mind
Sometimes rules should be left behind

The ward mouth has been on
Or knows somebody else who has been on
Or knows somebody else who knows somebody else
Who knows every medicine to treat cancer
The ward mouth has tried most things
Apart from herbal remedies and silly diets
So don't bore her by sharing your advice
She's not afraid to tell the Oncologist what to do
And then tell everybody else what to do too
She can't quite understand
what the overseas Doctor says
So she doesn't argue with him.
The ward mouth can't keep quiet
when maybe she should
Advising the nurses on her medication
and how to take her blood
She's been on these wards so many times
Her breasts, bones, lungs and brain
are all riddled with disease
There's not much left of her except her loud mouth
And, just occasionally, her fearful silence

The ward mouth always seems close to me
Sort of niggling in my ear all the time
I wonder
Could the ward
Mouth
Be
Me?

Nurses

Slope-shouldered, bellies before them
The nurses are coming, slowly of course
Soldiers they are, doing their job
They boss me around over bloods and other stuff
I watch them and try to imagine them in the buff
Anything to bring on a smile
Nurses they pat me, distracted
Then I hear them guffaw in another room
They have flat-footed footsteps
And very short memories

But I am the woman who won't just do what they say
The one who demands that you look her in the eye
Miss Shirty, I bet they call me
Why? Because I know my own veins
And when they come for me, I'm ready.